This book belong to

A is for

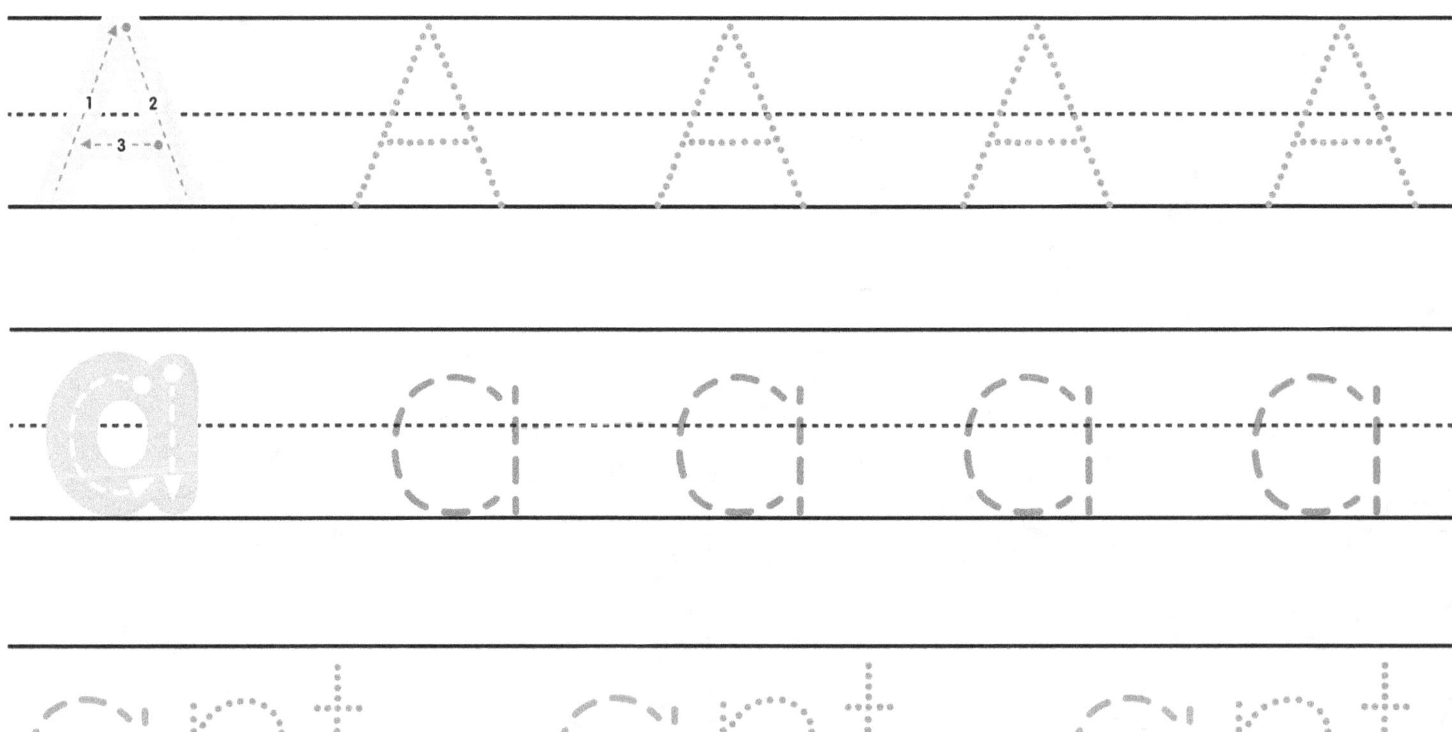

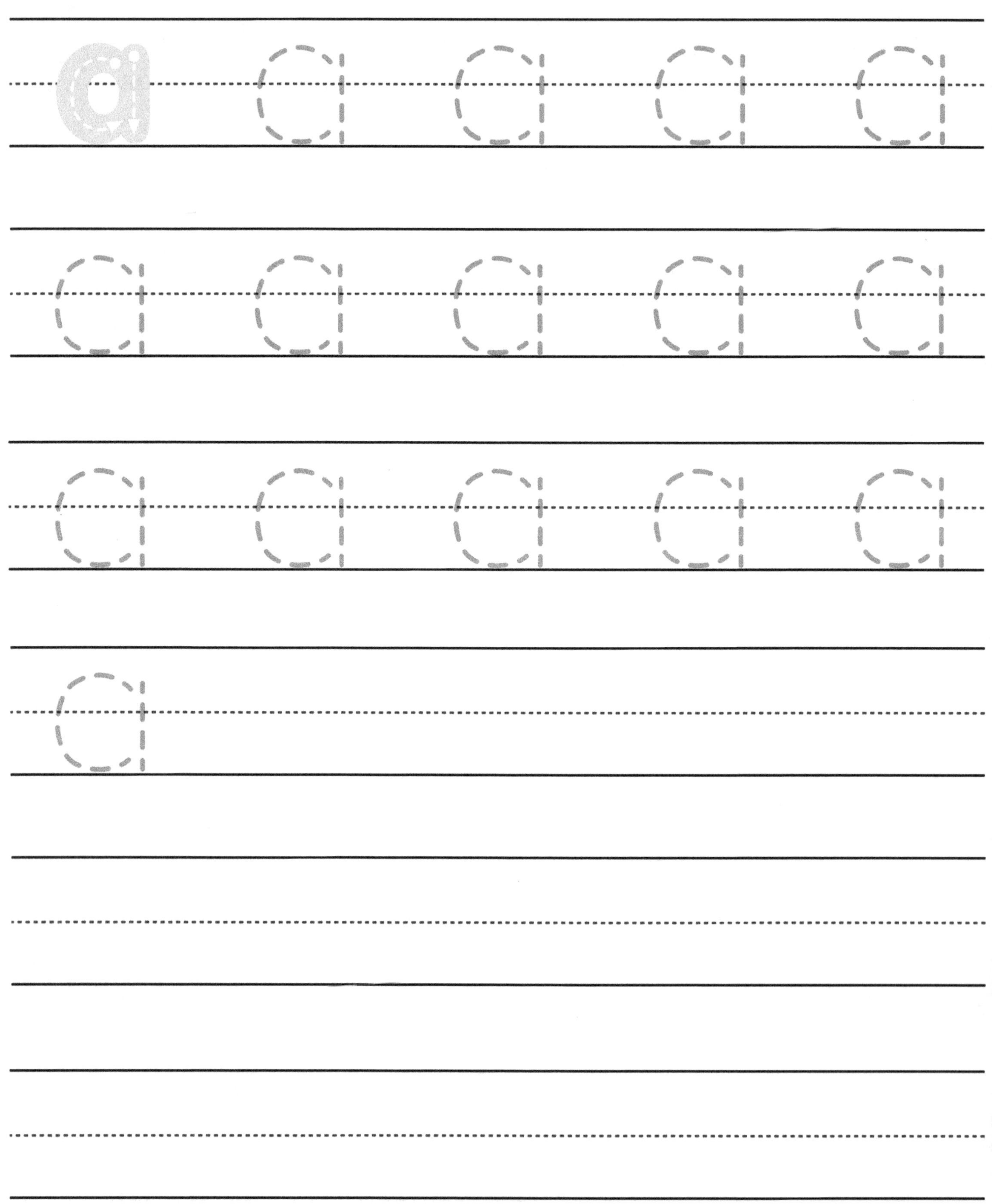

ant ant ant

ant ant ant

ant ant ant

ant

B is for

bird

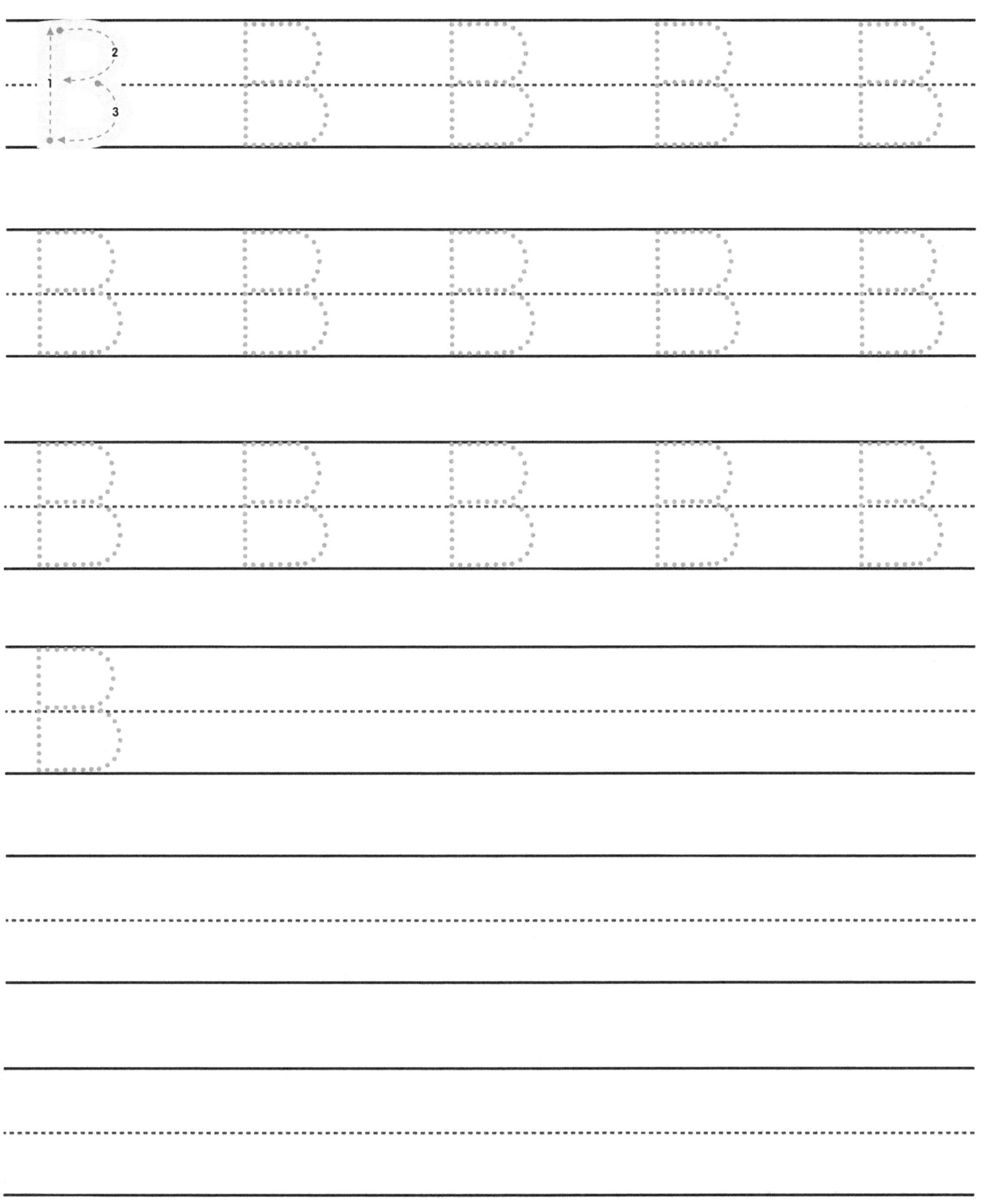

1

bird   bird

bird   bird

bird   bird

bird

C is for

cat

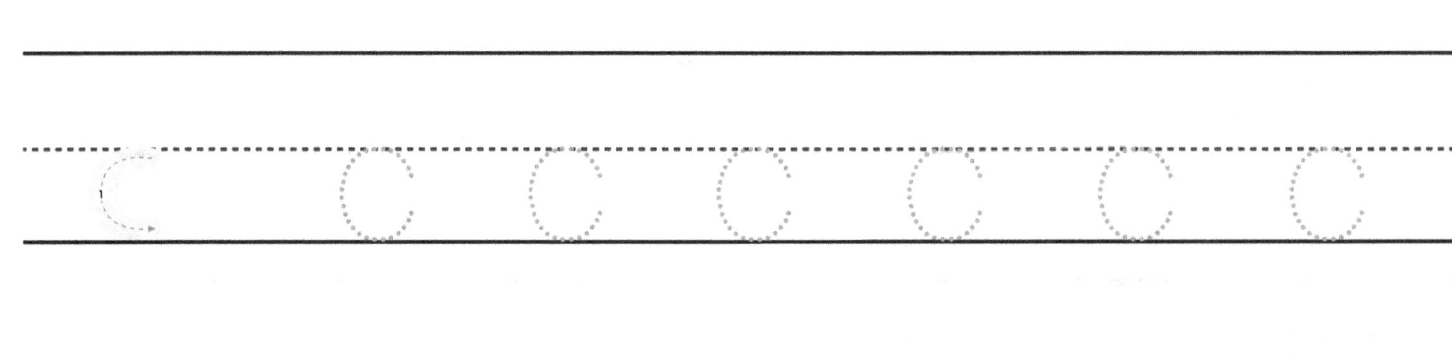

cat   cat   cat

cat   cat   cat

cat   cat   cat

cat

D is for

Dog

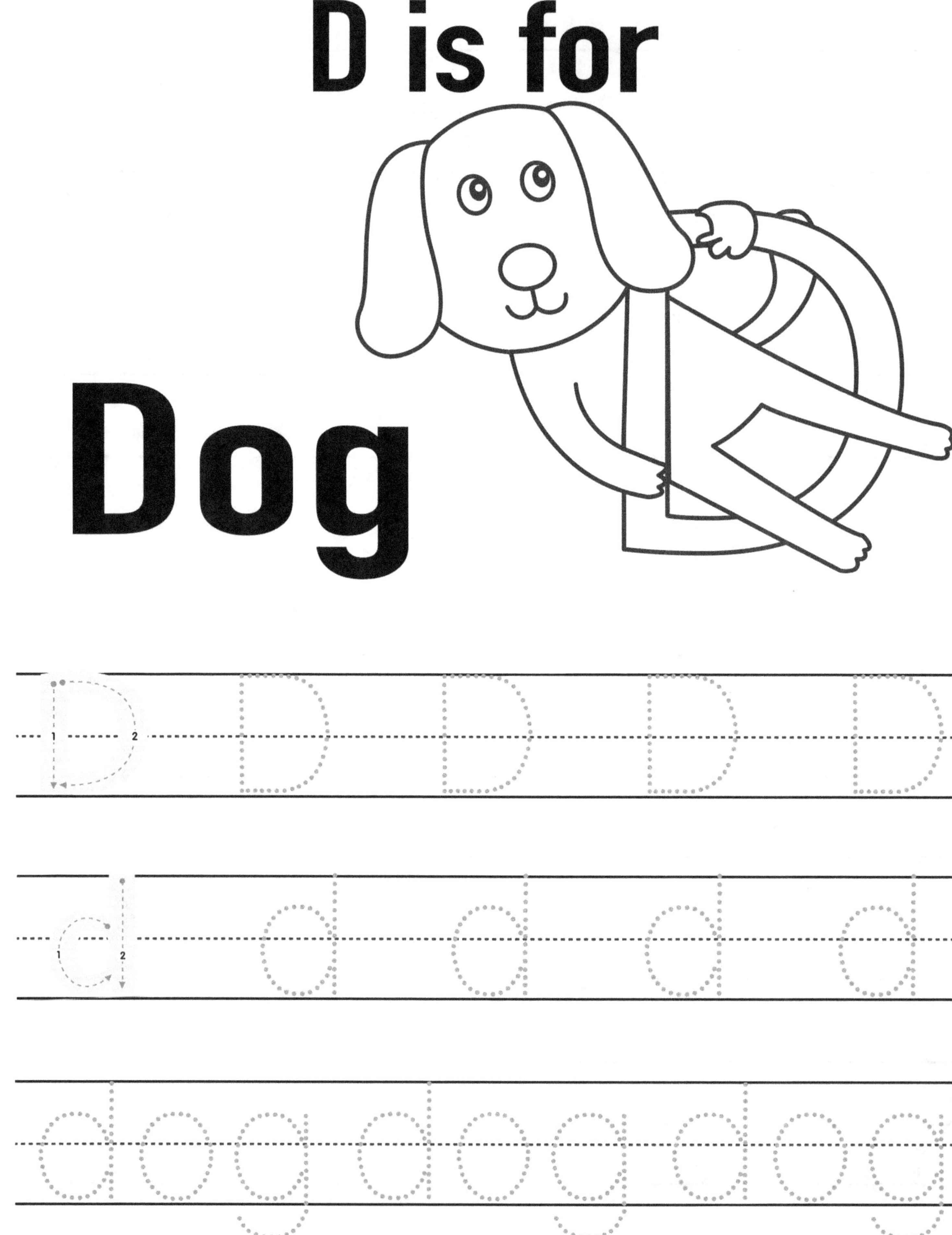

dog dog dog

dog dog dog

dog dog dog

dog

E is for

2
1 3
4

elephant
elephant
elephant

F is for

Frog

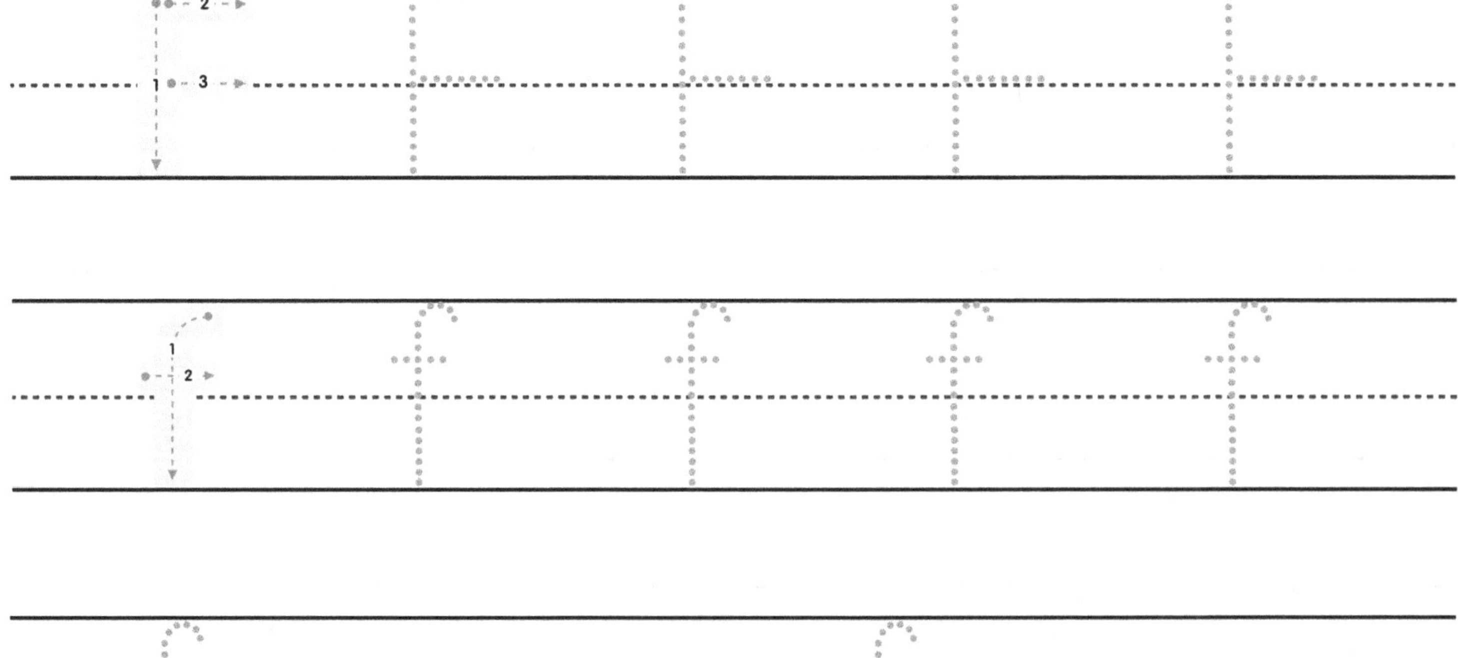

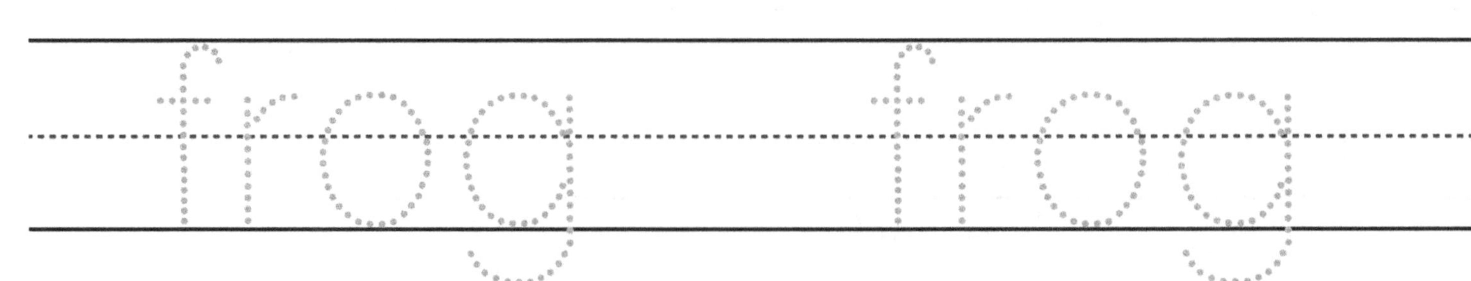

2

1 3

frog frog

frog frog

frog frog

G is for

Giraffe

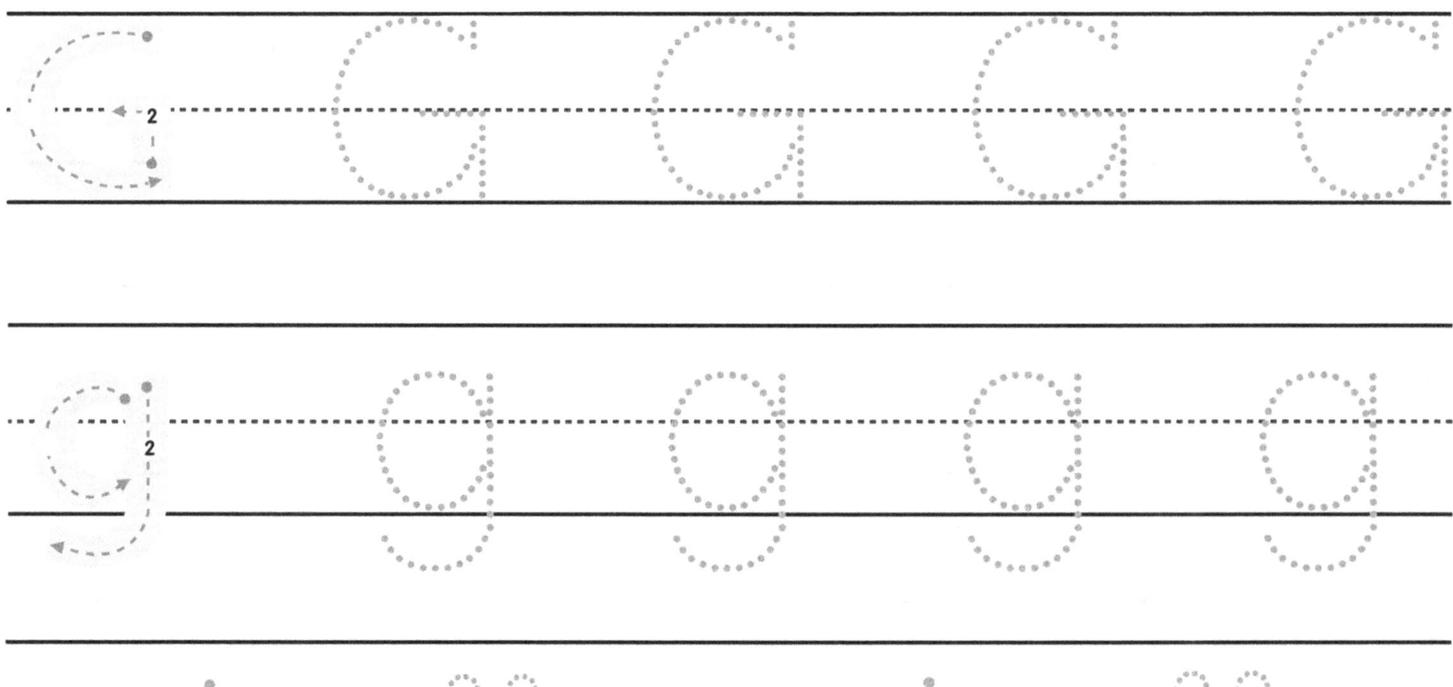

giraffe giraffe

giraffe giraffe

giraffe giraffe

H is for

Hippo

1
2
3

hippo hippo

hippo hippo

hippo hippo

I is for

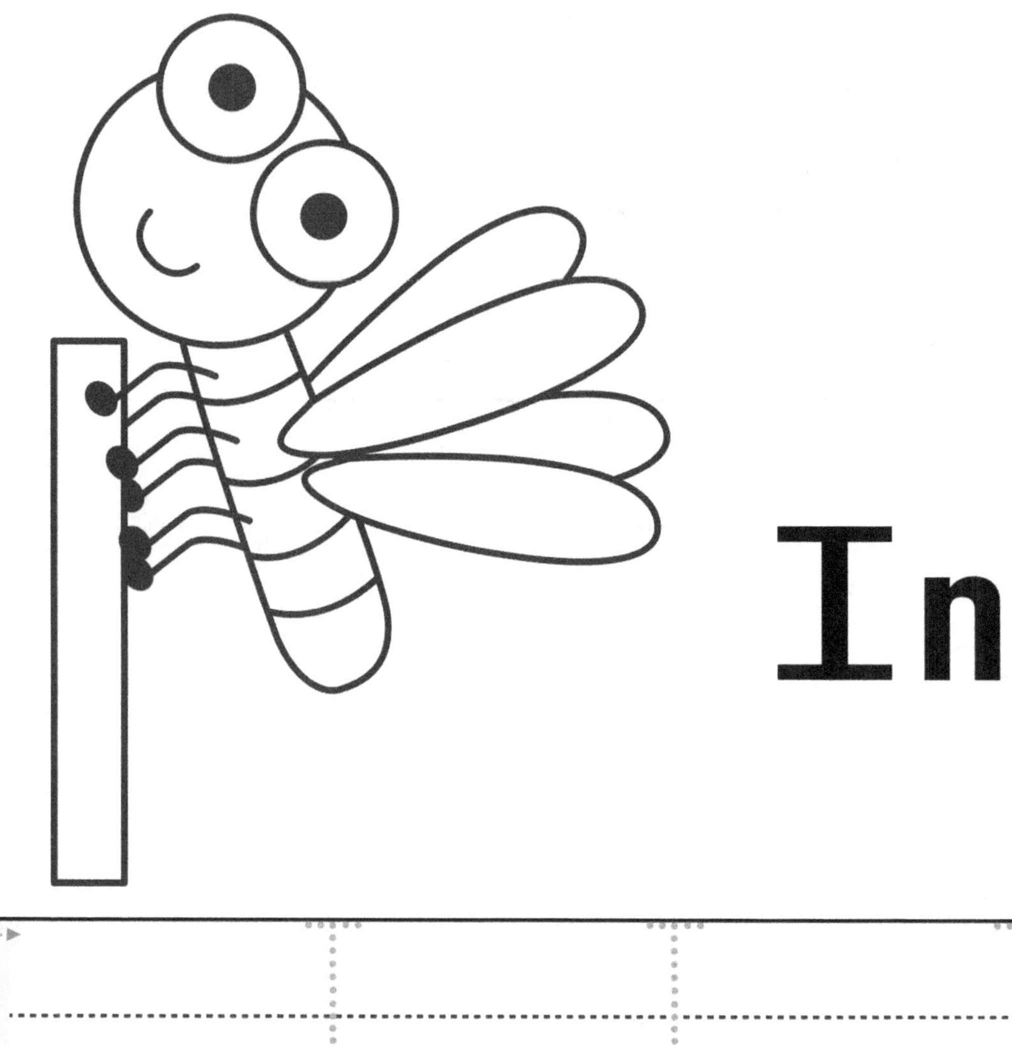

Insect

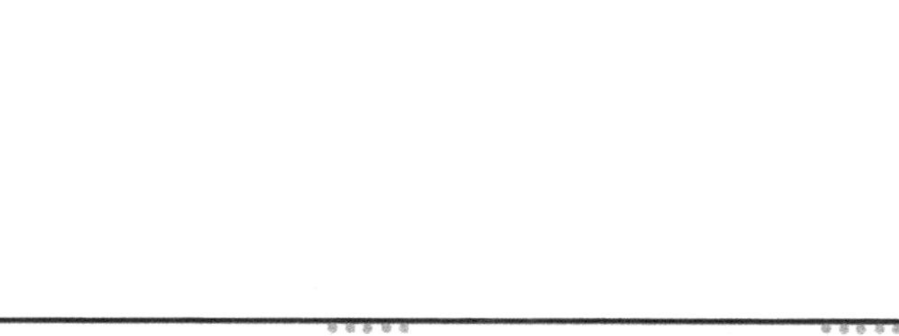

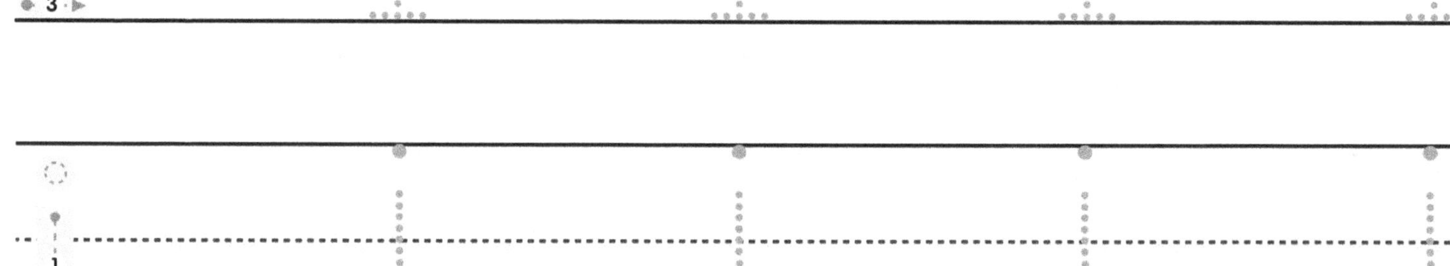

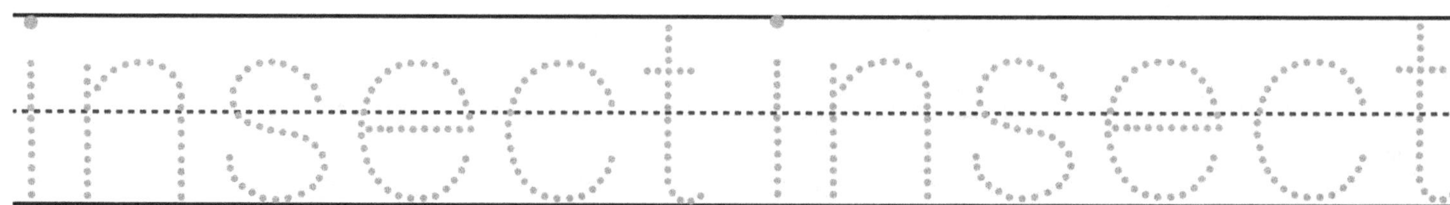

insect insect

insect insect

insect insect

J is for

Jnsect

jackal jackal
jackal jackal
jackal jackal

K is for

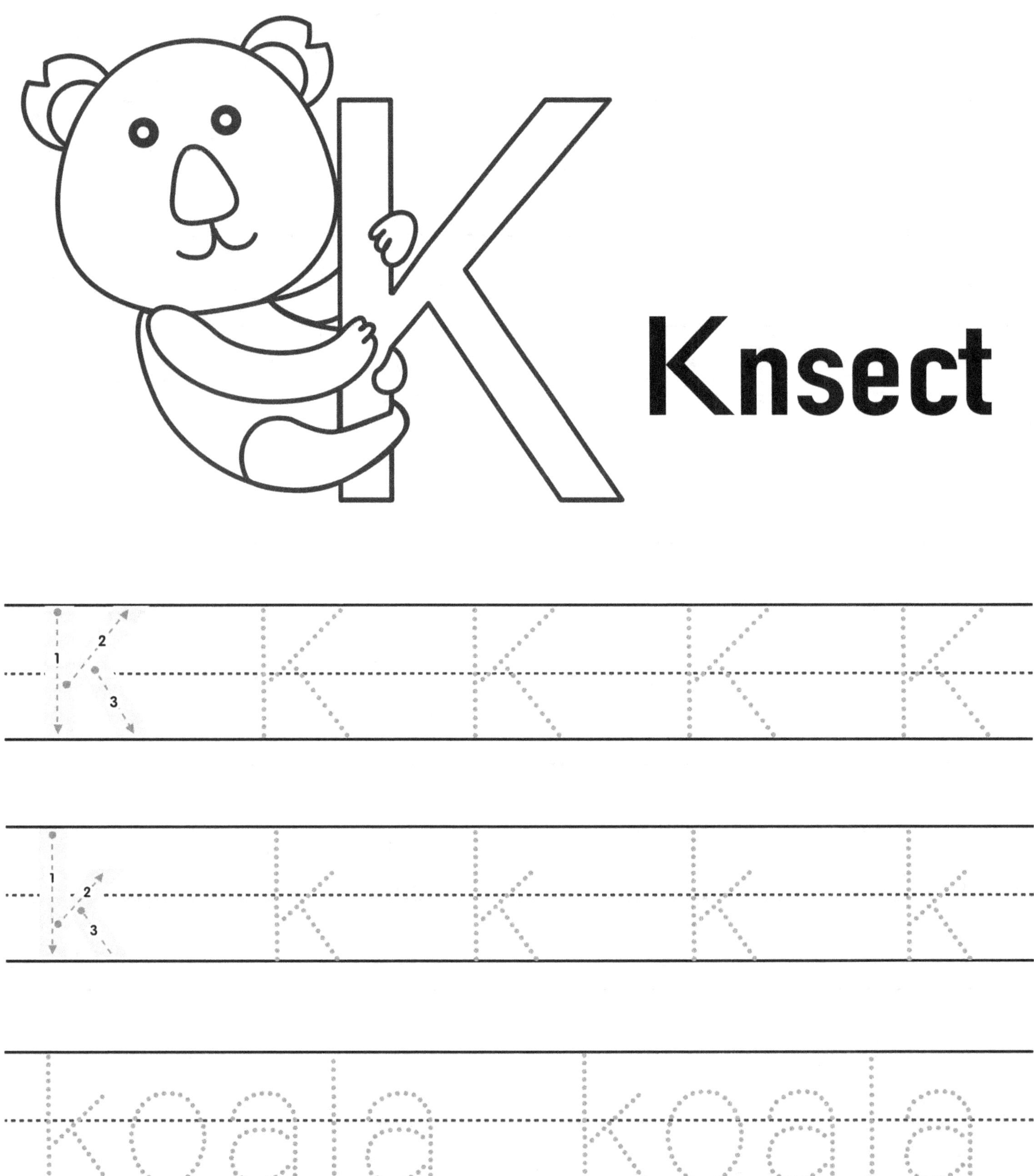

Knsect

koala koala

koala koala

koala koala

L is for

Lion

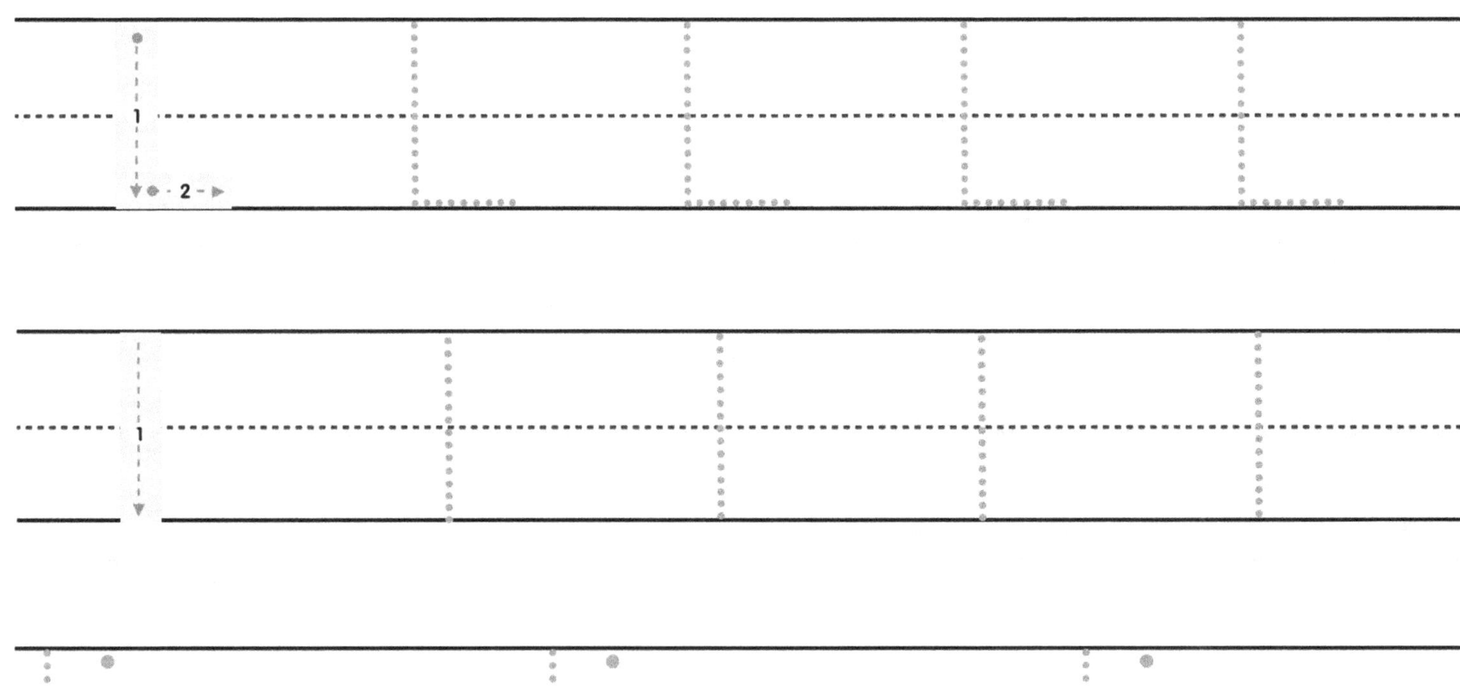

lion lion lion

lion lion lion

lion lion lion

M is for

Monkey

monkey

monkey

monkey

N is for

Newt

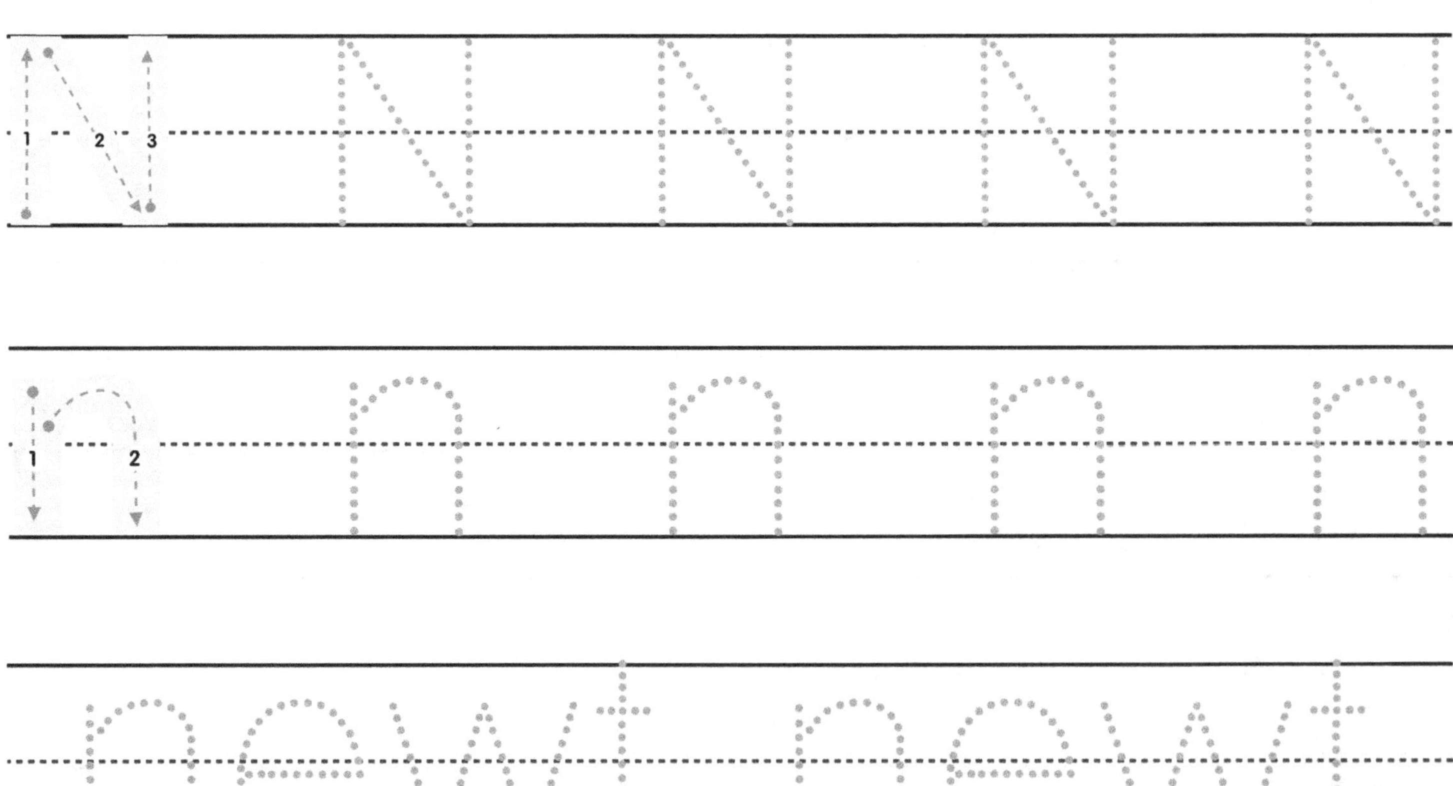

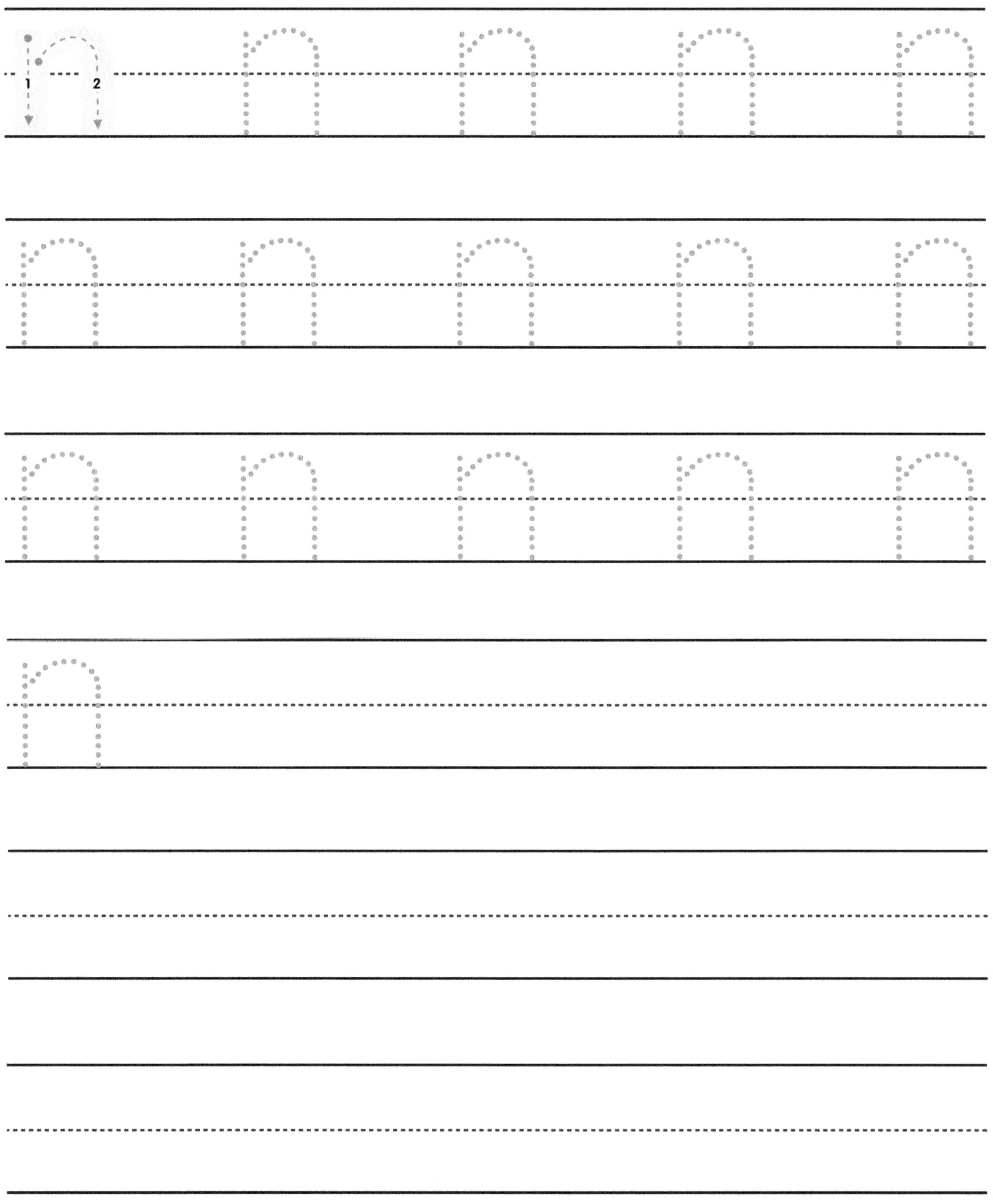

newt newt

newt newt

newt newt

O is for

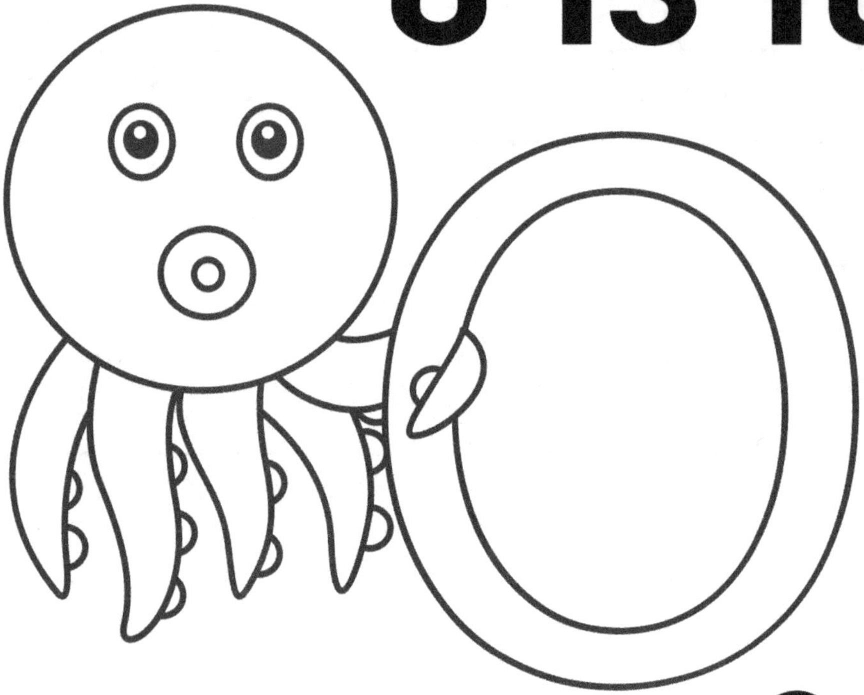

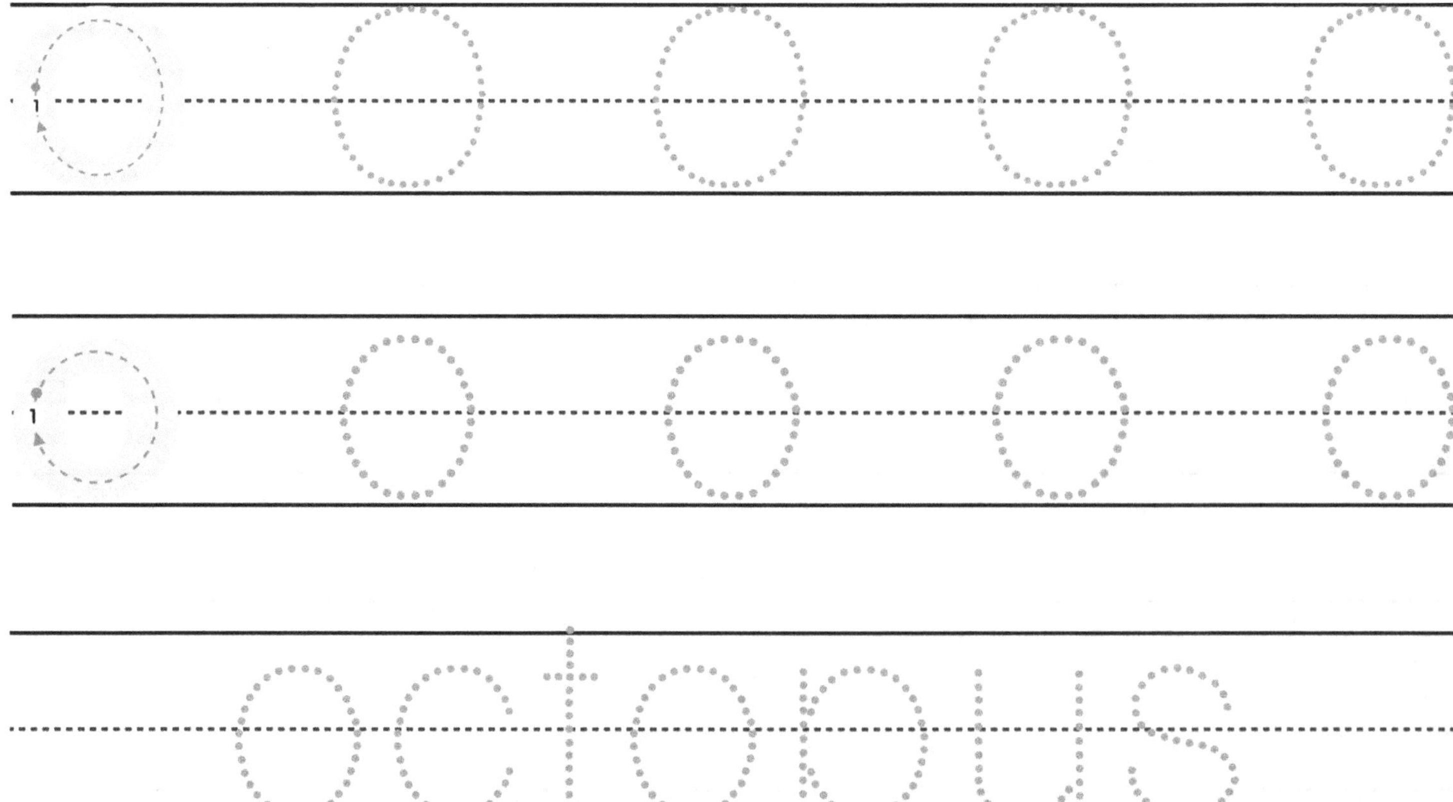

Octopus

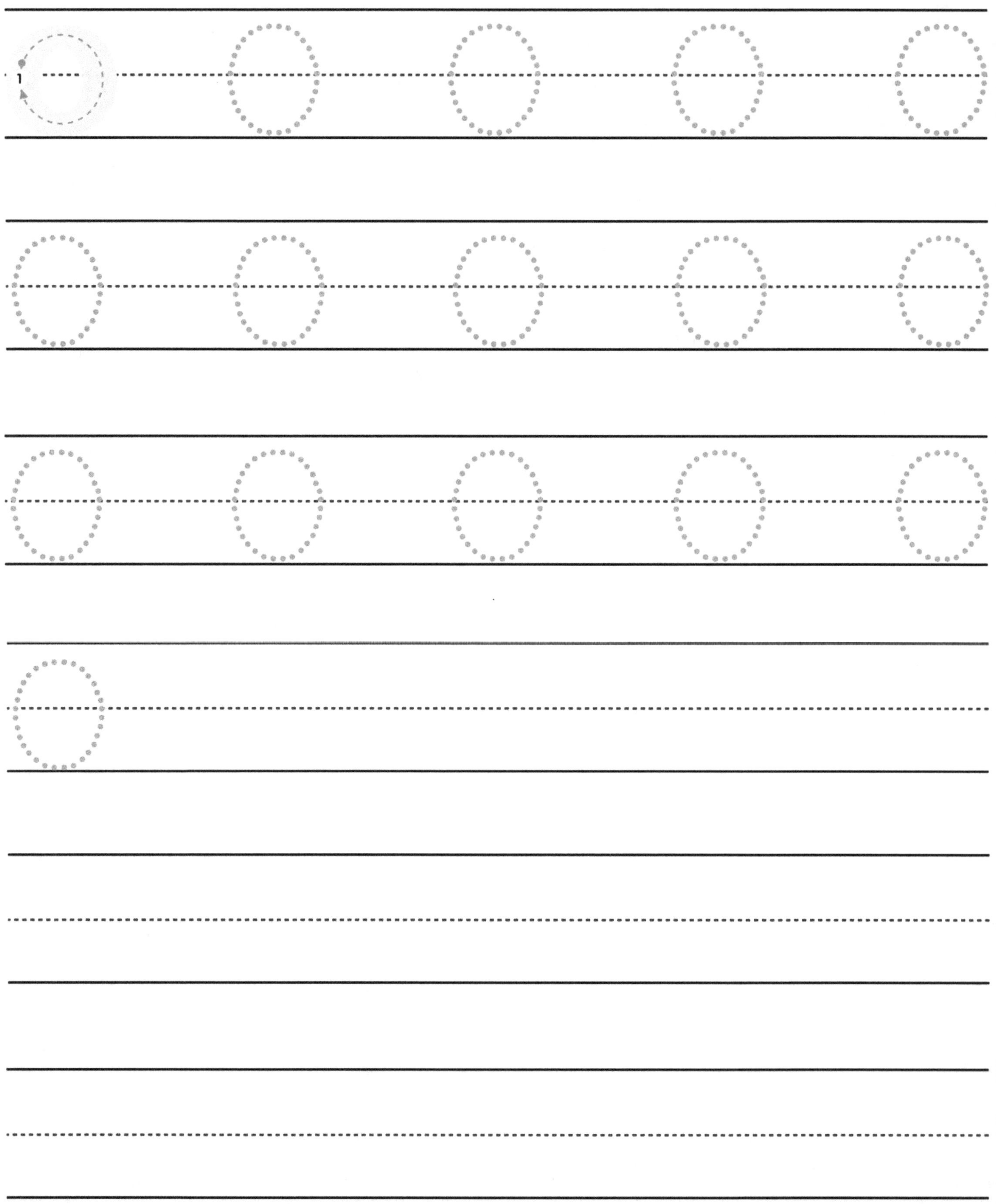

octopus
octopus
octopus

P is for

Panda

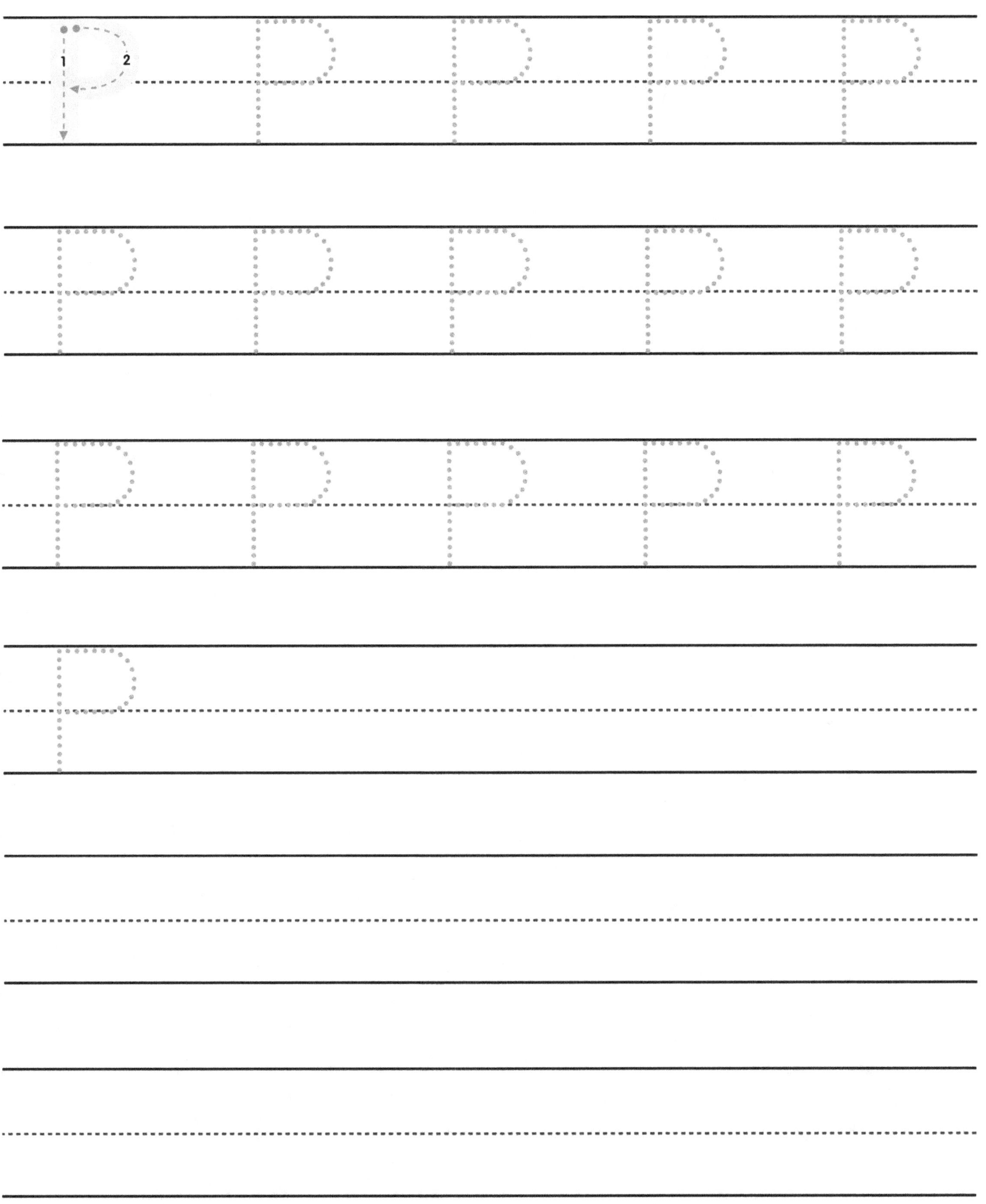

p   p   p   p   p

p   p   p   p   p

p   p   p   p   p

p

panda panda

panda panda

panda panda

Q is for

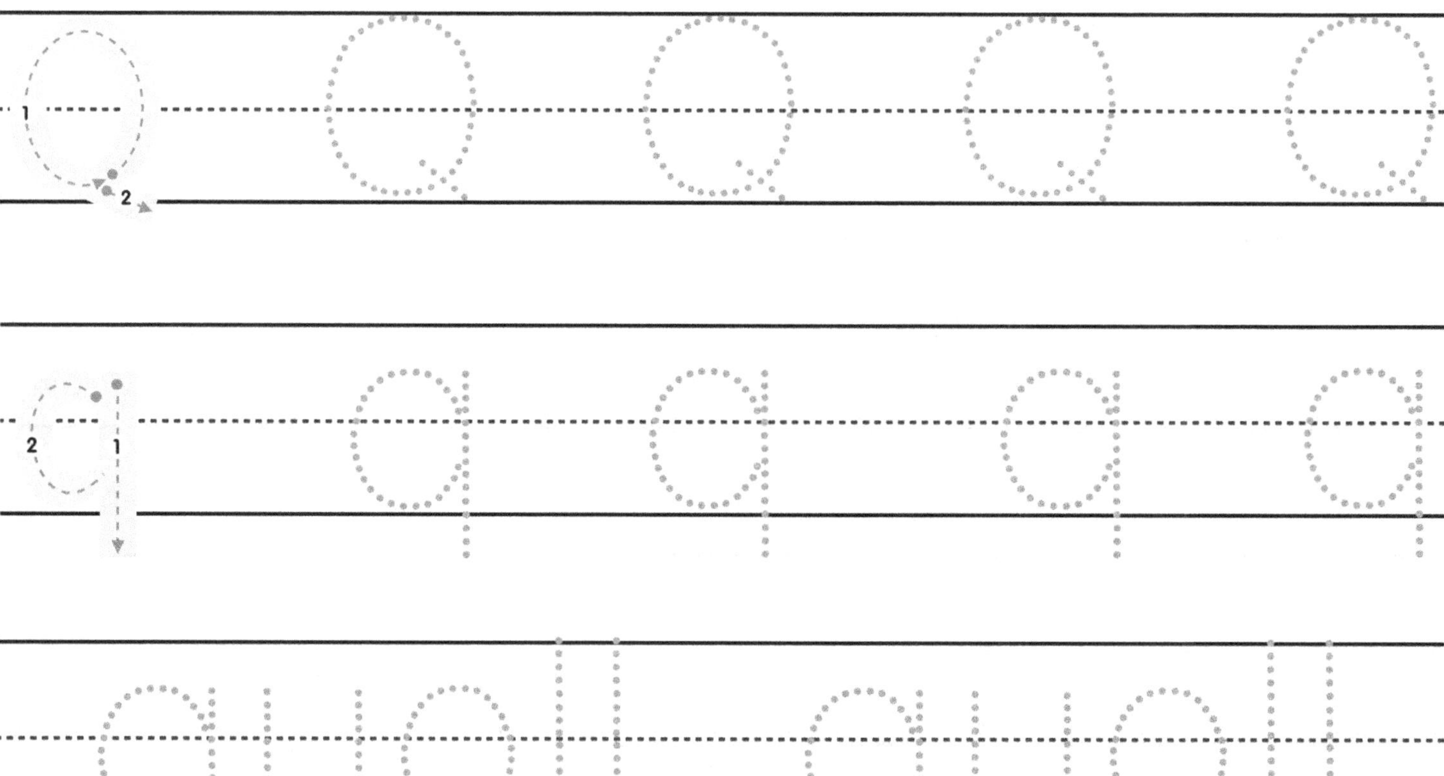

Quoll

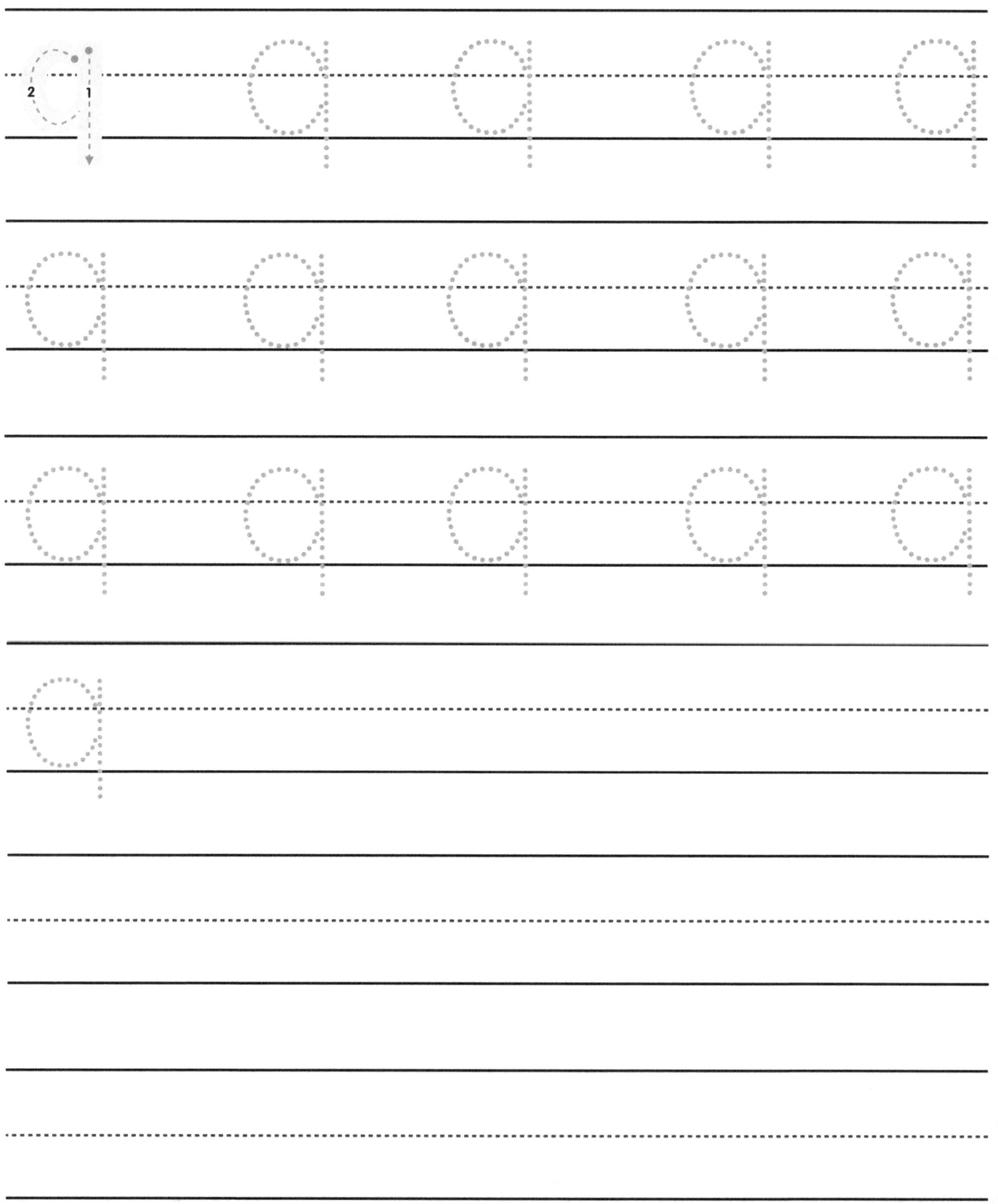

quoll   quoll

quoll   quoll

quoll   quoll

R is for

Rabbit

2
1

rabbit   rabbit

rabbit   rabbit

rabbit   rabbit

S is for

Sloth

S S S S S S

S S S S S S

sloth sloth

sloth sloth

sloth sloth

sloth sloth

T is for

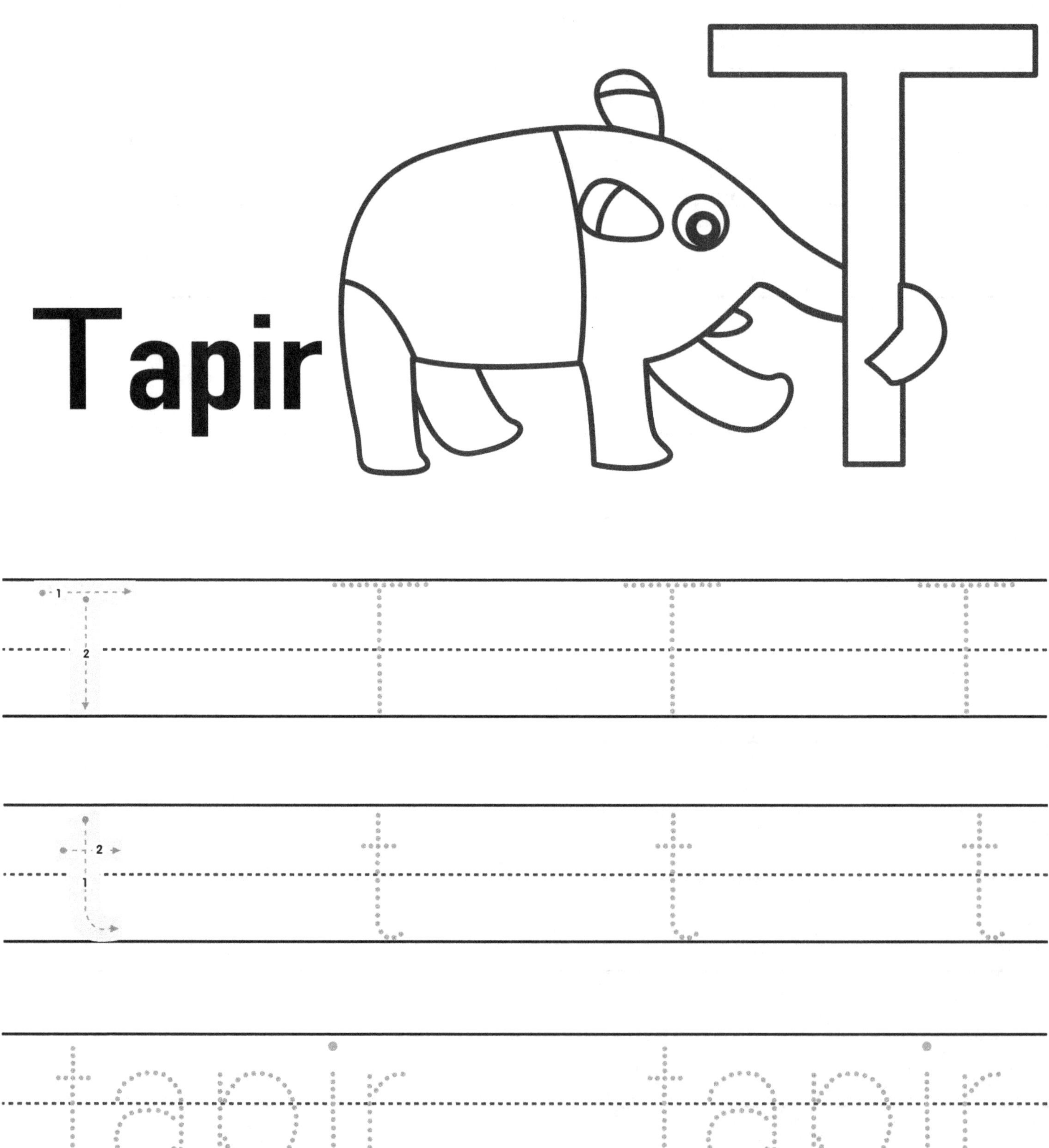

Tapir

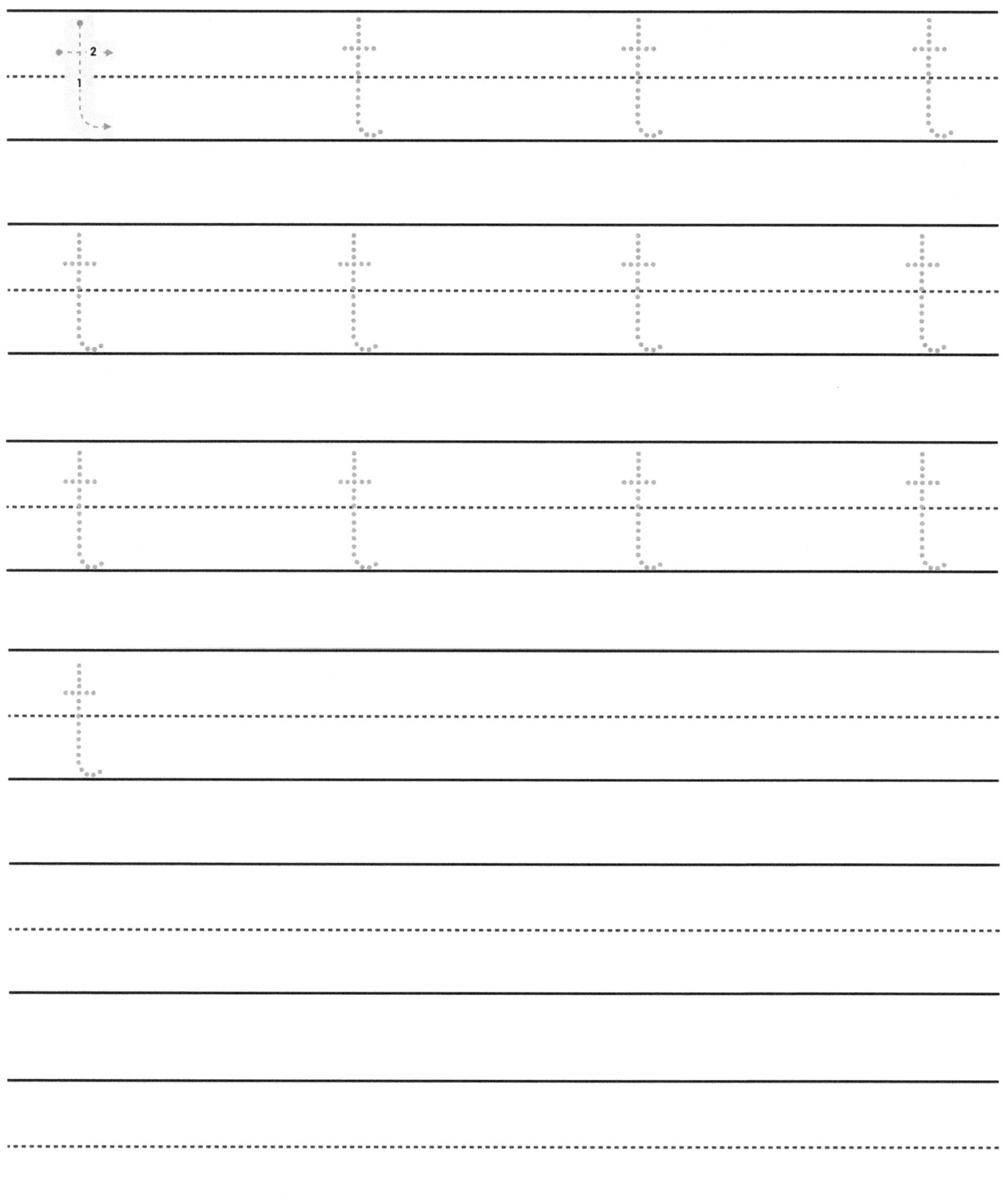

tapir   tapir

tapir   tapir

tapir   tapir

U is for

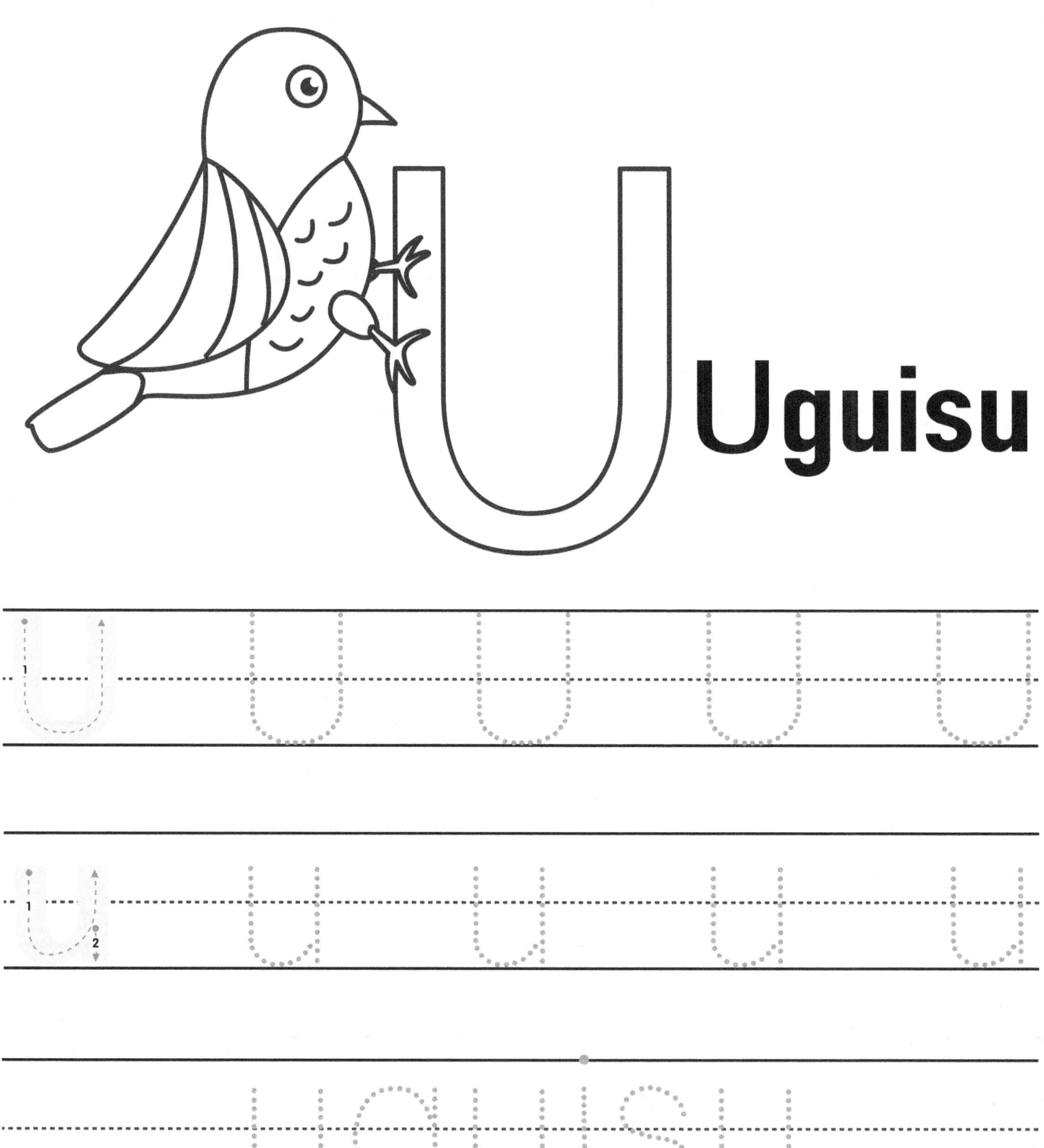

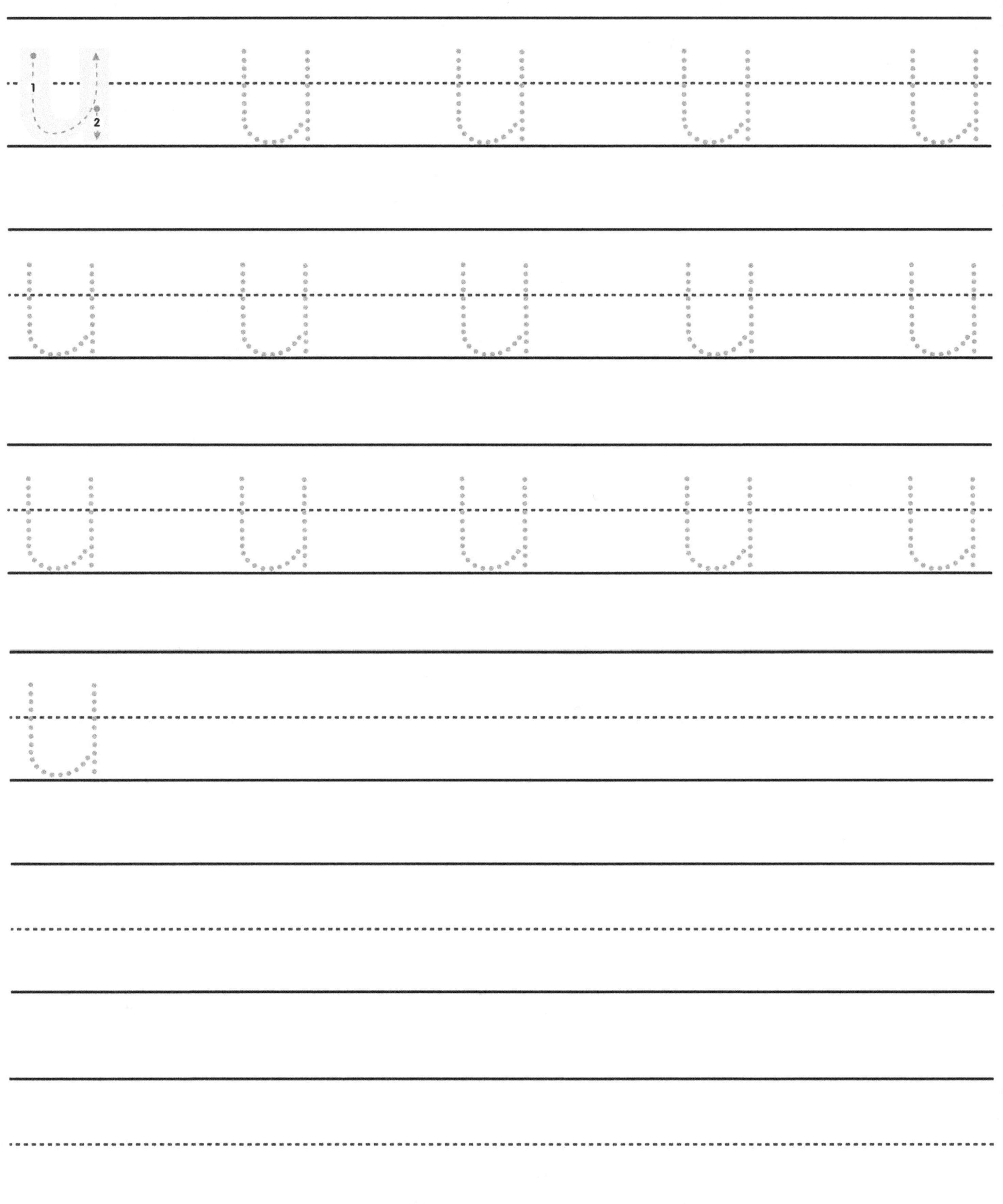

uguisu
uguisu
uguisu

V is for

Vervet
monkey

v v v v v

v v v v v

vervet mokey

vervet mokey

vervet mokey

W is for

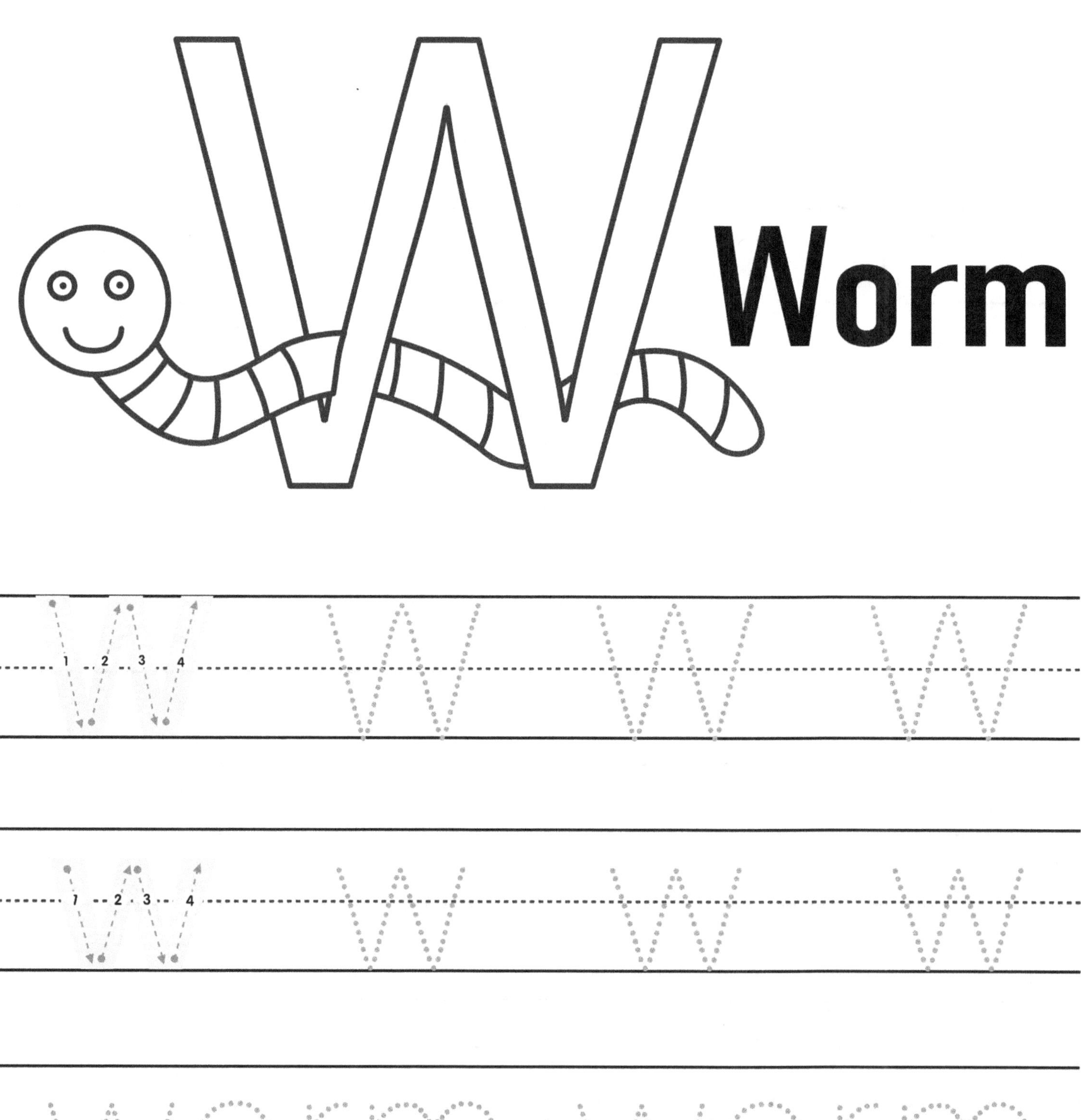

Worm

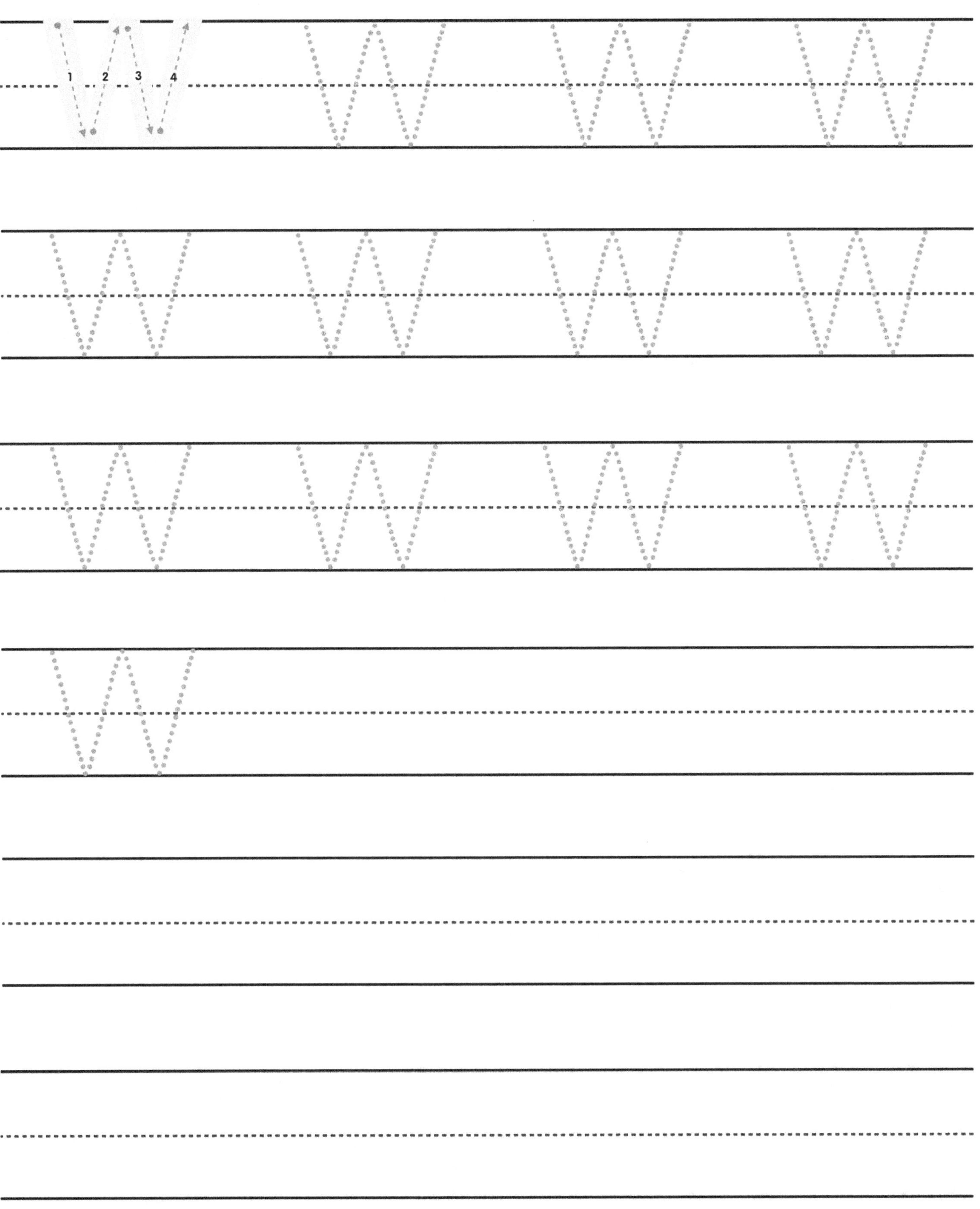

worm worm worm

worm worm

worm worm

X is for

Xerus

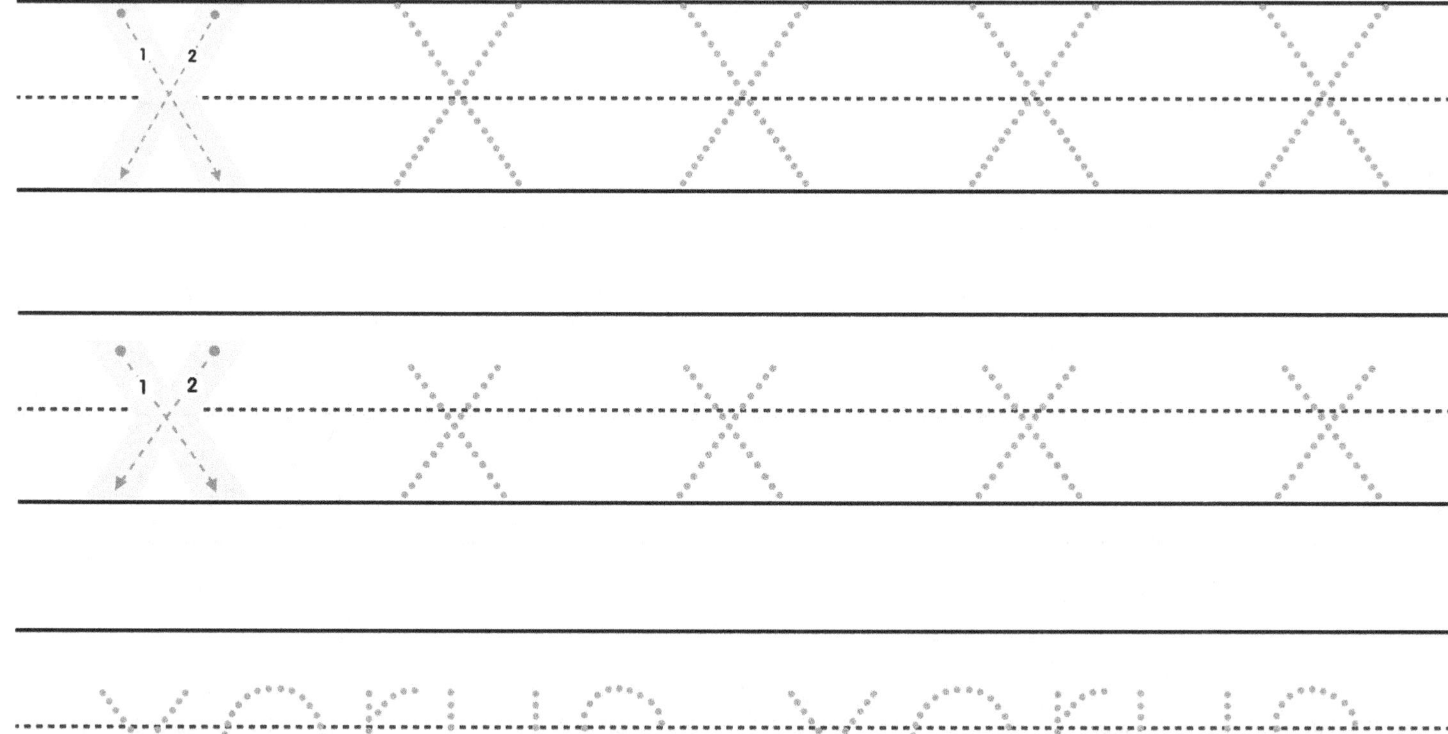

xerus xerus

xerus xerus

xerus xerus

Y is for

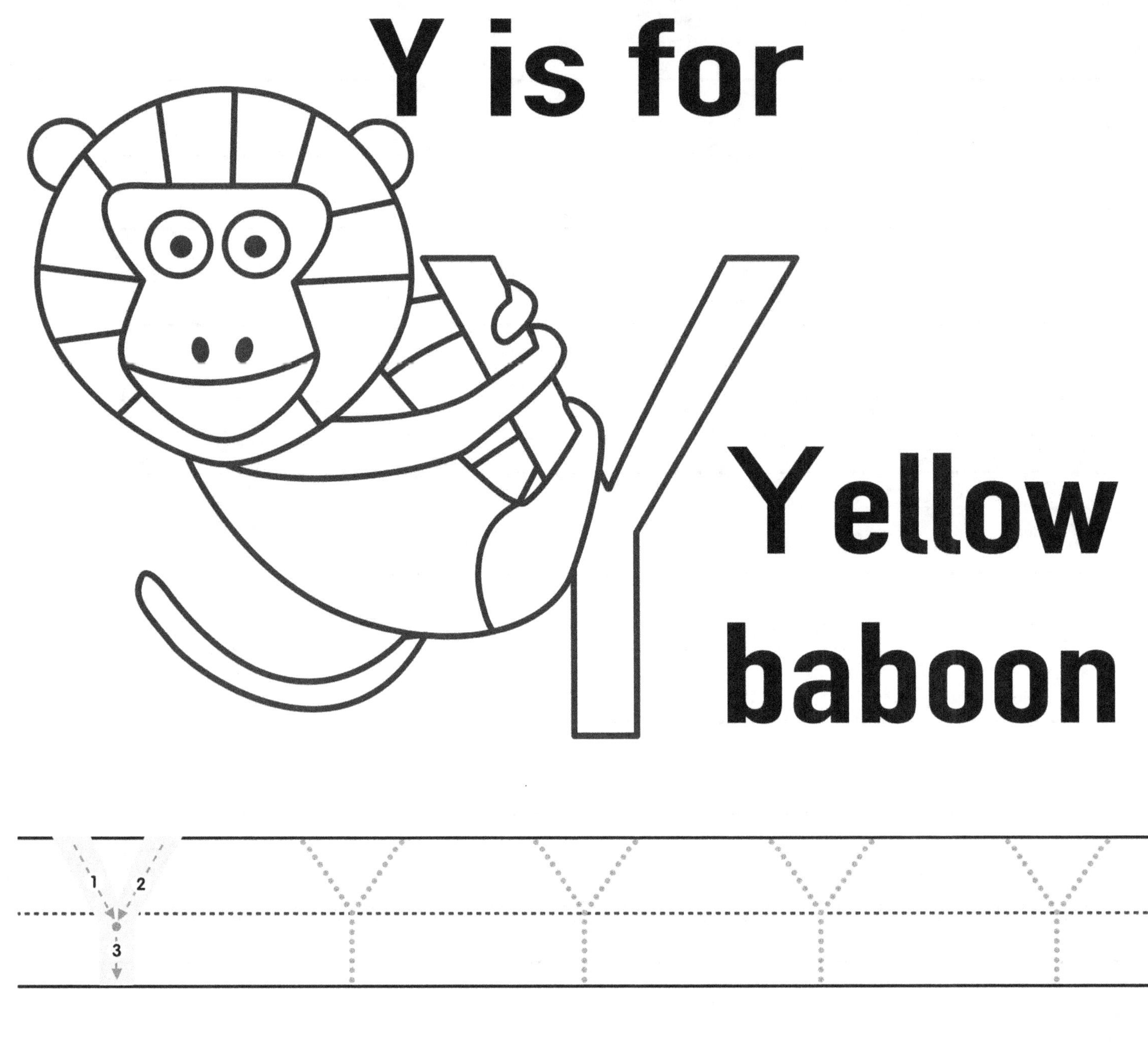

Yellow
baboon

yellow baboon

yellow baboon

yellow baboon

Z is for

Zebu

1

2

3

zebu zebu

zebu zebu

zebu zebu

www.ingramcontent.com/pod-product-compliance
Lightning Source LLC
Chambersburg PA
CBHW081951260726
48657CB00009BA/2663